HOPE COLLEGE

This is my Anchor of Hope for this people in the future.

Rev. Albertus C. Van Raalte

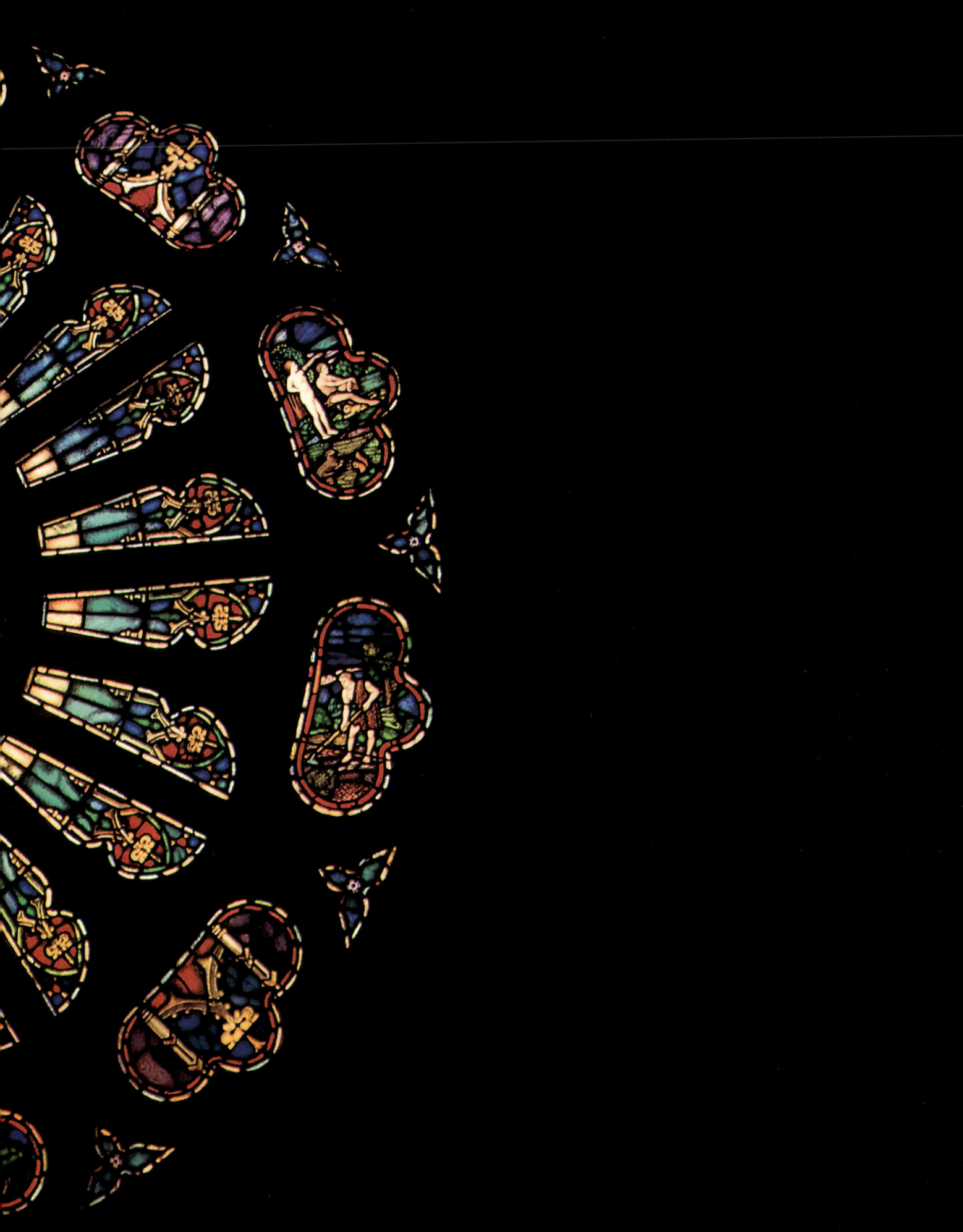

HOPE COLLEGE

PHOTOGRAPHY BY JOHN de VISSER

HARMONY HOUSE
PUBLISHERS-LOUISVILLE

The Reverend Albertus C. Van Raalte, Founder

Executive Editors: William Butler and William Strode
Library of Congress Catalog Number: 90-70919
Hardcover International Standard Book Number 0-916509-82-6
Printed in The Republic of Korea
through Vivid Color Separation, New York, New York
First Edition printed Fall, 1991 by Harmony House Publishers,
P.O. Box 90, Prospect, Kentucky 40059 (502) 228-2010 / 228-4446
Copyright © 1991 by Harmony House Publishers
Photographs copyright © 1991 by John de Visser

This book or portions thereof may not be reproduced in any form without
the prior written permission of Harmony House Publishers. Photographs may not be
reproduced in any form without permission of John de Visser.

Our thanks to the Hope College community for all its help in the production of this book,
especially Tom Renner, Director of Public Relations. We would also like to thank
Robert N. De Young, Vice President for College Advancement; Gregory S. Olgers, Assistant Director for
College Advancement; and Larry J. Wagenaar, Archivist of The Joint Archives of Holland.

Graves Hall

A CHRONOLOGY OF HOPE

1847 Settlements created in Michigan, Illinois, Wisconsin and Iowa by citizens from the Netherlands.

1848 "Holland" Michigan platted as a "Village."

1850 A "Tract of Land" later known as "The Five Acres," donated by the Rev. A.C. Van Raalte, and designated as a site for "The Academy."

1851 "The Pioneer School," the first educational institution in the new settlement, formally opened.

1853 The General Synod of the Reformed Church in America assumed control of the school.

1857 Van Vleck Hall erected on "The Five Acres."

1859 "The Five Acres" enlarged to 16 acres and designated "The College Campus."

1862 The first freshman class, 10 in number, matriculated.

1865 Philip Phelps, Jr. elected first president of Hope College.

1866 Charter of Incorporation as a College of Liberal Arts granted by the State of Michigan; First Commencement of Hope College.

1876 The Rev. A.C. Van Raalte died.

1880 Charles Scott elected provisional president of Hope College.

1886 Construction started on the President's Home (completed in 1896).

1892 Graves Library and Winants Chapel cornerstone laid.

1893 Gerrit J. Kollen elected third president of Hope College.

1903 Van Raalte Memorial Hall dedicated (destroyed by fire in 1980).

1906 Carnegie Gymnasium dedicated (renamed "Carnegie-Schouten Gymnasium" in 1954; razed in 1982).

1907 Elizabeth R. Voorhees Girls Residence dedicated.

1911 Ame Vennema elected fourth president of Hope College.

1918 Edward D. Dimnent elected fifth president of Hope College.

1929 The Memorial Chapel dedicated (renamed "Dimnent Memorial Chapel" in 1959).

1931 Wynand Wichers elected sixth president of Hope College.

1938 Hope Preparatory School, originally "The Pioneer School," discontinued.

1942 Science Building (later "Lubbers Hall") opened.

1945 Irwin J. Lubbers elected seventh president of Hope College.

1950 Formal opening of Winifred Hackley Durfee Hall, dormitory for women.

1956 Music Hall completed (named for the late John B. Nykerk in 1962). Kollen Hall opened.

1960 Phelps Hall dedicated.

1961 Van Zoeren Library opened (renamed Van Zoeren Hall in 1988).

1963 Calvin A. VanderWerf elected eighth president of Hope College. Fraternity Dormitory Complex and Gilmore Hall opened.

1964 Physics Mathematics Hall opened (renamed "VanderWerf Hall of Physics and Mathematics" in 1981).

1967 Dykstra Hall completed.

1969 Brumler House for apartment living dedicated.

1970 Wynand Wichers addition to Nykerk Hall of Music dedicated.

1971 DeWitt Student and Cultural Center opened.

1972 Gordon J. Van Wylen elected ninth president of Hope College.

1973 Peale Science Center opened.

1978 Dow Health and Physical Education Center opened.

1982 College East Apartments opened. DePree Art Center, a former furniture factory, dedicated.

1983 The 118th Commencement ceremony, the first held outdoors in the college's history, was conducted at Holland Municipal Stadium.

1986 Maas Student and Conference Center constructed.

1987 John H. Jacobson, Jr. elected 10th president of Hope College.

1988 The Holland Theatre downtown donated to the college and renamed and reopened by Hope as the Knickerbocker Theatre. Admissions House completed. Van Wylyn Library dedicated.

1990 Dedications for Van Andel Plaza, the Paul G. Fried International Center, Van Zoeren/VanderWerf and the DeWitt Center for Economics and Business Administration.

Lubbers Hall

Voorhees Hall

PREFACE

Hope College has much for which to be grateful — an involved, caring family of alumni, parents and friends, a committed faculty, students of fine quality, and a beautiful physical plant. All these elements, and others, come together to make each year an exciting adventure in learning and personal growth for all involved.

With the college's 125th anniversary at hand, it is especially appropriate that we see just who we are and where we've been. Often we are so busy living our lives that we forget to take the time to reflect upon them. As I review the images collected for this volume, I am overwhelmed by how active and vital a place Hope College is.

I invite you to immerse yourself in the images contained in this book. Most are recent, a few are quite old, but grounded as each is in the locations, traditions and dreams of those of previous years, they all testify eloquently to the success of the legacy left by the Reverend Albertus C. Van Raalte and those who shared his vision in a settlement carved out of the wilderness by Dutch pioneers so many decades ago.

Sincerely,

John H. Jacobson

Dr. John H. Jacobson
President of Hope College

INTRODUCTION

There is a wonderful dichotomy in the way in which colleges are both exceedingly temporal and eloquently timeless.

An institution such as Hope measures its generations in fleeting, four-year increments, from the "birth" of one freshman class to the "birth" of the freshman class that succeeds it when it leaves, and for each group of graduates the college's existence is contained neatly within the confines of their undergraduate careers. As they leave Hope behind, they take with them the issues and ideas, the victories and defeats, the encounters and sentiments, that gave their time at the college substance. With the taking, moreover, they leave those who replace them, the new freshmen, a blank slate upon which to record their own memories and experiences, unencumbered by their predecessors' perceptions.

Hope College is more, however, than the disjointed sum of the experiences of those who have come and gone in a cycle that is as regular and predictable as the coming and going of the seasons. Unquestionably, there is a Hope Experience, an Experience that is recreated each time a class enters the college and passes through; an Experience that is shared by classes even far removed in years.

Part of the universal Hope Experience lies in the physical situation of the college. Hope is — and has always been — located just a few blocks south of downtown Holland, set amidst the city's quiet, tree-lined, residential streets. Much of the landscaping and many of the physical facilities postdate generations of graduates (like Van Wylen Library, dedicated in 1988), but there are some constants that have served as landmarks since the college's beginning — such as Van Vleck Hall, constructed nine years before the college received its charter in 1866, and the seemingly-primeval Pine Grove. Other buildings almost qualify, like Graves Hall, completed in 1894, or the President's Home, finished in 1896.

Beyond its transient physical self, however, Hope possesses the character that has marked it since its beginning. Like the physical dimensions of the college, that character has evolved, but the core remains.

Hope has since receiving its charter maintained a lasting commitment to providing an education in the context of the historic Christian faith. The expression of that commitment has changed through the generations, but the commitment itself has been a constant influence on the nature of the college.

Founder Albertus C. Van Raalte, discussing the Object of the college in the *Hope College Circular* of June 17, 1857, stated, "Any student having in view the office of a teacher, a minister, or a missionary will be welcomed at the school — It is at all times necessary to dispense a thorough education to the youth that they may become worthy members of society. The doors of this institution will ever be open to the deserving of all classes, with the hope that many be trained here who shall become ornaments to society, and pillars of the State."

Even today Hope prepares many future teachers, ministers and missionaries, but much emphasis is now placed on other fields as well. Whatever the role the college's graduates intend to play, however, they all receive the benefit and perspective provided by an education that incorporates faith as an implicit, if not explicit, part of learning.

Hope is a place of caring — an aspect of the college's Christian commitment. Faculty members, for example, extend their interest in their students beyond their academic work. Many students, in turn, dedicate themselves to activities that will benefit others — such as volunteering to help build homes for the needy, or as Big Brothers and Big Sisters.

The college has also long been a place of academic integrity and excellence.

Hope is one of only seven insitutions in Michigan able to grant its students admission to Phi Beta Kappa — the highest academic honor an undergraduate in the United States can receive. A recent report places Hope in the top three percent of America's 867 undergraduate institutions in the proportion of graduates who, since 1920, have gone on to earn doctorates. Possession of a terminal degree should in no way be regarded as an indication of a person's worth, either extrinsic or intrinsic, but such studies are considered a valid means of judging an undergraduate institution's academic performance.

Armed with the preparation they received at Hope, graduates of all generations have gone on to distinguished careers. Alumni serve as capable business and government leaders, dedicated physicians, respected clergy and committed college educators. The quality of their education is a shared heritage of which all can be justifiably proud.

There are doubtless other examples, but those outlined serve to illustrate that the memories of Hope retained by the college's many graduates, regardless of their era, reflect the place in which they occurred. There is a bond of context that unites the graduates of all ages, no matter how different the college appeared, or how different their immediate concerns were. Their memories may not be precisely the same, but they are remembering, in some ways, precisely the same things.

The images in this book depict the Hope experience — the Nykerk and Christmas Vespers participants, the action of the Hope-Calvin basketball game, the graduates and parents on graduation day. In sharing the experiences of a recent graduation, however, this book shares the enduring Hope College Experience as well: the Hope Experience of Christian commitment and academic excellance; of traditional events and new inquiries; of brisk West Michigan winters and warm friendships on a friendly campus.

Remember the Hope Experience through the shadows of these recent Hope experiences, and enjoy the images of Hope contained on the pages which follow. They are your past. They are Hope's future.

Spera in Deo.

Gregory S. Olgers
Thomas L. Renner
Larry J. Wagenaar
December, 1991

Van Vleck Hall

Overleaf ; The President's Home

Van Zoeren Hall and Van Wylen Library

*And now, from all our future time,
As thro' life's maze we go,
Be this our motto, brothers all!
Spera tu in Deo!
Yes! Hope in God, when it is dark,
And hope, when it is light!
For hope shall never cease to be,
Till lost in perfect sight.*

Rev. Philip Phelps, Jr.
Commencement Ode, 1866

The Liberal Arts College emphasizes the education that has for its purpose the development of the intellectual and spiritual values in human life in striking distinction from all other values.

Dr. Edward D. Dimnent

Lubbers Hall

Dewitt Center

Dewitt Center

My faith is in God who founded Hope College that it may produce men and women to do His work in the world.

Dr. Wynand Wichers

It is my firm conviction that Hope College can serve this day and generation only by inculcating upon young lives those virtues and values which have been the hallmarks of the Christian scholar.

Dr. Irwin J. Lubbers

Dow Center

A Hope College liberal arts degree is not an end in itself, but the opening of a door to a life of learning and significant living.

Dr. Calvin A. VanderWerf

The mission of Hope College is to offer, with recognized excellence, academic programs in liberal arts, in the setting of an undergraduate, residential coeducational college and in the context of the Christian faith.

Dr. Gordon J. Van Wylen
Hope College Mission Statement

Christmas Vespers

65

De Zwann Windmill

What we do here has significance in itself, but it also has a significance that goes beyond Hope.

Dr. John H. Jacobson
Fall Convocation, 1988

Big Red Lighthouse

ewitt Center Theater

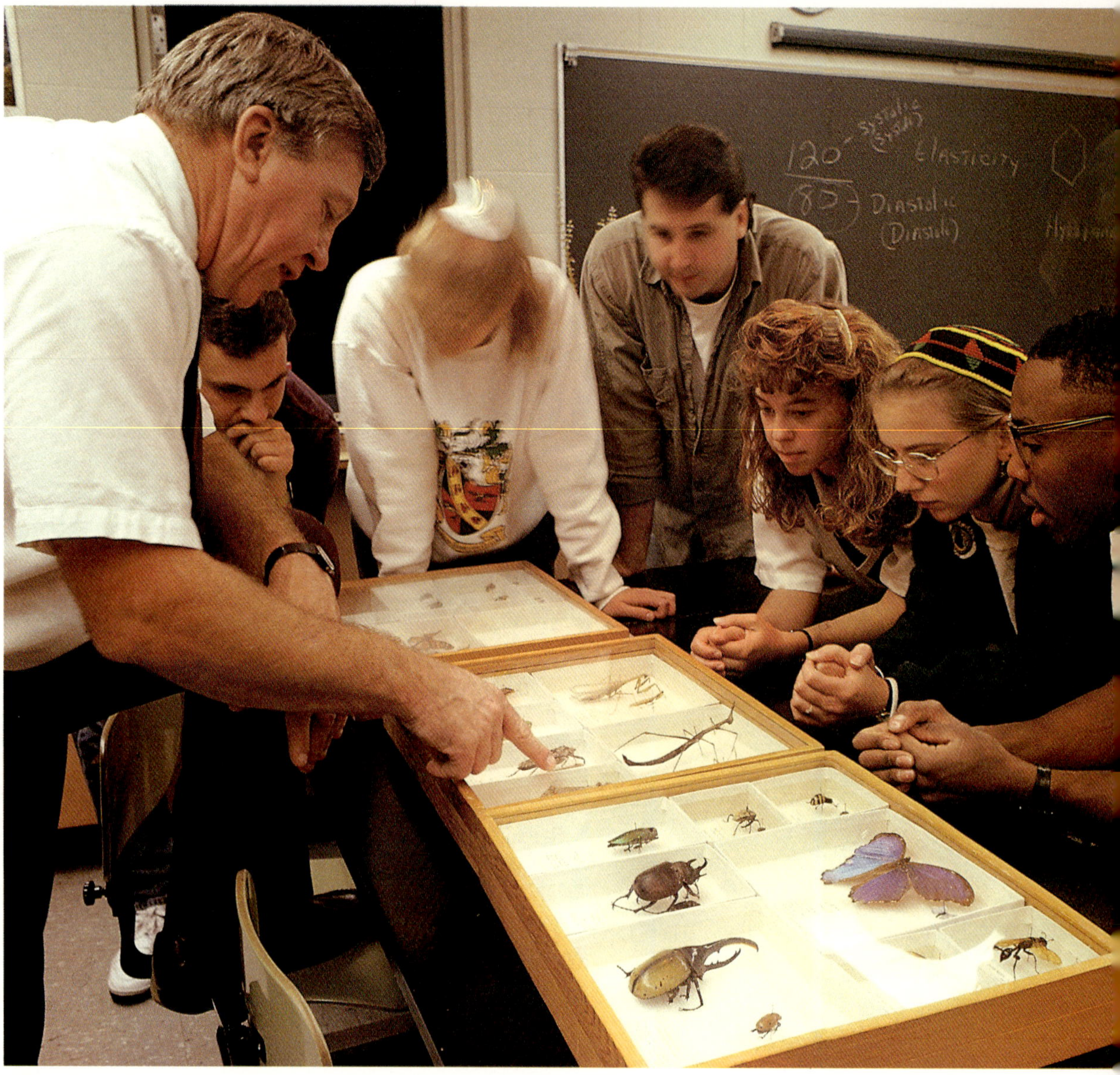
120
Systolic
Elasticity
85
Diastolic

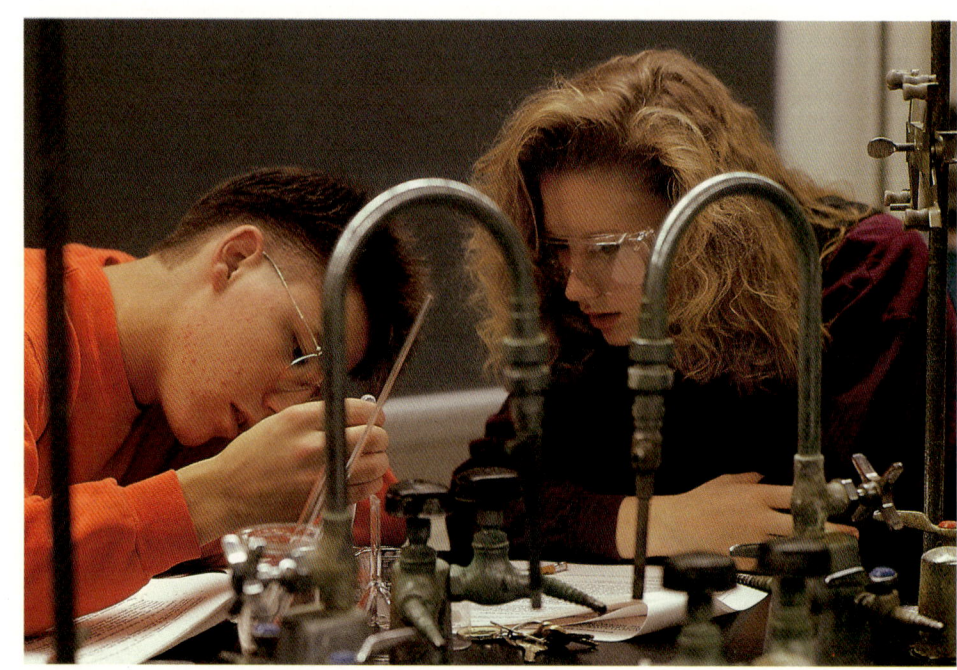

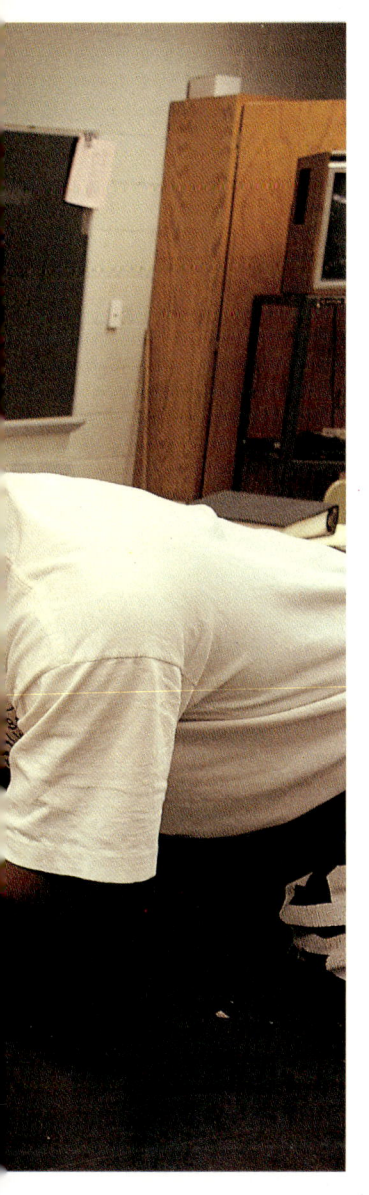

75

HOPE COLLEGE
A 125th Anniversary Retrospective

featuring
A selection of images from the Joint Archives of Holland

Compiled by Larry J. Wagenaar, Archivist

This view of Hope's campus was drawn about 1890. It shows the entirety of the campus at the time and the prominence of Van Vleck Hall.

This is my anchor of Hope for this people in the future.
Rev. Albertus C. Van Raalte

Albertus C. Van Raalte brought a group of Dutch settlers from the Netherlands and started the Holland colony on the banks of Black Lake. He had a strong commitment to education and in 1851 helped organize the Pioneer School and later was involved in the founding of Hope College. Hope was incorporated on May 14, 1866, two months before the first commencement.

In 1862, with student labor and direction, a gymnasium was constructed to the east of Van Vleck. This building also served as the chapel and a community meeting place. One Hope graduate wrote, "we all followed him [President Phelps] out to the forests, felled the trees, rolled the logs to the river and they were floated down to old Pluggers Mill, thence sawed into lumber for our projected building."

After a flurry of correspondence, Albertus Van Raalte persuaded John Van Vleck to come and direct the Pioneer School, which was renamed the Holland Academy. He served as the third principal of the school. It was during his four-year tenure (1855-1859) that Van Vleck Hall was constructed.

Van Vleck Hall served as the focal center of the campus for nearly half a century. Miraculously, the building was one of the few structures to survive the devastating fire which burned 80% of Holland in 1871. Similar fires throughout the Midwest, including the great Chicago fire, strained resources and made rebuilding materials scarce.

Rev. Philip Phelps served as the first president of Hope College from 1866 to 1878. The school struggled to make ends meet in the early years and survived a financial crisis brought on in part by the panic of 1873. Five professors made up the faculty in the school's first year.

While Hope was growing, so was the Holland community. This picture, taken in about 1890, shows the growing downtown area. Fewer than forty years earlier this street would have had a handful of stores and numerous tree stumps from the original forests. *(Photograph from The Holland Historical Trust Collection of The Joint Archives of Holland.)*

Gerrit J. Kollen served as Hope president from 1893-1911. As the college grew new things were added. The *Milestone* was launched as a single edition in 1905, and became an annual beginning in 1916. During this period students became active in organized athletics and the Pull became an annual event.

One of the significant buildings of the first decade of the 20th century was Carnegie Gymnasium. Gerrit Kollen developed a relationship with Andrew Carnegie and persuaded him to fund the construction. It was one of the only non-libraries he built.

Graves Hall was constructed in 1894 with a gift from Nathan F. Graves and Garret E. Winants. Winants Auditorium served as the chapel until 1929 and later as the library until the construction of Van Zoeren Library in 1961. Graves was constructed of locally-quarried Waverly stone.

A.C. Van Raalte was commemorated in the construction of a large four-story structure in 1903. A monumental building for its time, it towered over the sparse campus. Van Raalte Hall was destroyed by fire in 1980 and the grassy area where it stood is now known as Van Raalte Commons.

A photo of an early football team, circa 1910. Often old photographs are formal but, as this photo shows, students in that day could have fun, too.

The Dickensian Society, a literary society similar to fraternities on campus, having a bit of fun.

Much like the honorary and departmental groups of today, students formed groups around their area of interest.

Women were also active in college sports. Above is the 1905 women's basketball team.

The *Anchor* started in 1887 as a student-run publication. Through 1914 it was a pamphlet-type of publication with literary articles as well as news. The Archives has a full run of *Anchors* and they are often used in documenting Hope's history. This photo of the *Anchor* staff was taken in 1913.

The choir was and is an active part of many students' lives on campus. Here Dr. John Nykerk is seen with the choir in Winants Auditorium.

Dr. Edward D. Dimnent took over the helm of the college from Rev. Ame Vennema in 1918 and served until 1931. In addition to the presidency, he served at various times as a professor of Latin, Greek, Business and Economics beginning in 1897.

Organized competitive athletics came into their own in the early part of the century. Hope defeated teams that the college would not play today, such as the University of Michigan. This basketball team from the 1919-20 school year was victorious against the "Farmer Five" of the Michigan Agricultural College (later Michigan State University).

The Gothic style of the new chapel added a new dimension to the buildings on the campus. High points of the chapel include the Skinner organ, a gift of Bernard Arendhorst Sr., and the Rose Window given by the Class of 1916.

One of Hope's academic strengths is its natural science division which was supported by this building until the Peale Science Center opened in 1973. In 1975 the building was renovated for the humanities and social science divisions and renamed Lubbers Hall after President Irwin J. Lubbers, who served from 1945 to 1963.

Moving from Winants into the Memorial Chapel meant that there was much more space. Worship experiences have always been an important part of student life. Chapel attendance was mandatory until 1970.

Female students enjoying life in the dorms, 1938.

Fraternities and sororities have played a significant role in the history of Hope College. This is the Cosmopolitan Fraternity, taken circa 1924.

Homecoming was — and still is — a big event. Here a float is targeting DePauw in the 1951 Homecoming parade.

Professors line up for Baccalaureate in 1956.

Not all education took place on the Hope campus. Students have been encouraged to study abroad, as seen here taking in the sights of Europe in 1955. The Vienna Summer School, one of Hope's off-campus programs, was initiated in 1956.

Hope College students had national exposure on television's "College Bowl" circa 1963.

May Day has always been a highlight of the spring term at Hope College. Here the 1961 Hope May Queen, Roberta Russell, walks the royal path with her attendants at her side.

May Day festivities once included the obligatory May Pole shown here in 1964.

With the growing student population came the need for more buildings on campus to accommodate them. The Van Zoeren Library shown here was dedicated in 1961. Other buildings completed during this period include the Nykerk Music Hall, Kollen Hall and the Math-Science Building later renamed Vander Werf Hall.

In 1964, Hope's baseball team won the Michigan Intercollegiate Athletic Association

As the student population grew, the college needed more residential space. Here the fraternity complex to the east of Western Theological Seminary is under construction in 1962.

Calvin A. Vander Werf served as eighth president of Hope College from 1963 to 1970.

International students have a long tradition at Hope. Japanese students first attended here in the 1870s, and the current program with Meiji Gakuin University is nearly three decades old. Pictured here is the second group of students from Meiji Gakuin in 1965.

Hope has encouraged cultural diversity among its students. The Black Coalition, pictured here in 1973, is active on campus.

The Shakespeare Marathon in 1962 benefitted students in India. The sign says that they insisted on a minimum of $1 an hour for their late-night commitments.

Part of college fun was the Kangaroo Court, a sort of end to freshman orientation. Silly offenses against upperclassmen resulted in mock punishments.

Nykerk is an annual fall competition between freshman and sophomore women, and held in the Holland Civic Center.

Each spring the Chapel Choir engages in a tour. Here the choir visits the White House in 1970.

Many famous people have visited the campus including the queen of the Netherlands. Here Eldridge Cleaver is lecturing in 1977.

In the fall of 1972 football fever gripped the campus as the team tried to take another MIAA championship. They were finally successful in 1973.

Dr. Gordon Van Wylen assumed the presidency of Hope College in 1972 and served until his retirement in 1987. Van Wylen presided over phenomenal growth in both the number of students and the physical plant. He brought with him a dedication to liberal education in the context of the Christian faith.

One of the many extra-curricular activities is the college radio station. First a closed circuit and AM station known as WTAS, it now broadcasts in FM (89.9) to the college and area community as WTHS.

Following in the long and rich traditions of Hope College is Dr. John Jacobson, tenth president of the school. He assumed his position in 1987.

The faculty of Hope College in 1910-11. Three presidents are part of this photo. Gerrit J. Kollen is seated at the desk, Edward Dimnent is standing second from the left and a young Wynand Wichers is standing third from the left in the back row.

Photographs taken from The Hope College Collection of The Joint Archives of Holland except where noted.